A MOLLY MAGUIRE TRAGEDY

Hand of Innocence

TRUE STORY OF THE MOLLY MAGUIRES AND THOMAS P. FISHER

Thomas E. McBride
Betty Lou McBride

For information or orders contact:

The Old Jail Museum
c/o Thomas McBride
128 W. Broadway
Jim Thorpe, PA 18229
570-325-3309
TheOldJailMuseum@verizon.net

Printed by
Christmas City Printing Co.
Bethlehem, PA 18018

~ Acknowledgments ~

Thanks to the miners known as the Molly Maguires for their hard work and dedication to justice.

Many thanks to the Dimmick Memorial Library in Jim Thorpe and the excellent staff for assisting with my research.

Special thanks to our daughter, Kathleen McBride Sisack, for her assistance in putting this book into final form.

Thomas E. McBride
July 1, 2013

The material in this book was obtained from the
original handwritten trial transcripts

Commonwealth of Pennsylvania
vs.
Patrick Gildea
March 1872

Commonwealth of Pennsylvania
vs.
Thomas P. Fisher
December 11, 1876

~ CONTENTS ~

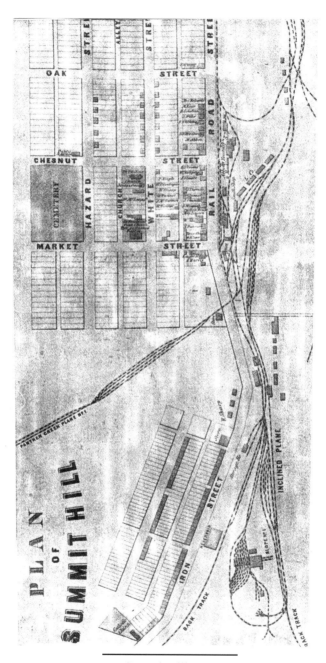

Summit Hill 1854
(Beers Atlas - Dimmick Memorial Library)

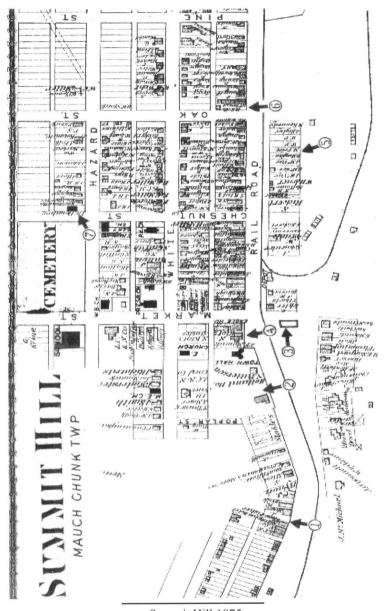

Summit Hill 1875

1 - Fisher's Rising Sun Hotel
2 - Site of Morgan Powell shooting
3 - Lehigh Coal & Navigation Co. office
4 - Klotz's Hotel

5 - Morgan Price Home
6 - Sweeney's Bar
7 - Dr. Donohoe's Office

(Beers Atlas - Dimmick Memorial Library)

~ *Chapter I* ~

Gildea and Brislin

The small town of Summit Hill located in northeast Pennsylvania, was bustling with activity in spite of the severe cold
and darkness. Warmly dressed families were hurrying by. Strollers
were on their way to visit friends and enjoy an evening's conversation. Miners covered in coal dirt were slowly trudging home after
laboring in the damp and dismal mines for twelve long hours which
had begun at six o'clock that morning. As usual, many of the
men of the town, including the weary miners, were dropping in at
a local store or bar to socialize and warm up their weary bones.
Some men stopped at Williamson's Dry Goods and Grocery Store,
while a few blocks away men of the Irish community stopped into
James Sweeney's Bar.

Over 80 years before this fateful day, Summit Hill had found
itself in the midst of a changing world. One magnificent, local
discovery was to become a catalyst to the Industrial Revolution,
eventually raising the standard of living and finally propelling the
country into greatness—in February 1791 Philip Ginder discovered coal. The daunting challenge of removing the valuable black
diamonds from the ground, securing shipping to commercial mar-
kets and establishing the importance of anthracite coal would not

happen immediately. Several years after coal was discovered, the Lehigh Coal and Navigation Company [LC&N] began both the mining and transporting of coal. The LC&N, realizing it would require many laborers to operate a coal mine, began to erect buildings around the coal mine. The first structure built was a large home for the mine superintendent, soon followed by smaller homes for the miners. Eventually a church, a school for the children and buildings for stores were erected. This small community became known as Summit Hill. The number of workers in the mine increased and by 1860 Summit Hill had become a thriving community of over 4,000 men, women and children. The LC&N also continued to grow, and by 1861 the company owned and operated 10 mines in the area.

Saturday, December 2, 1871 - 6:00 p.m.

On this dark, cold night several men talking together in Williamson's Store [134 W. Ludlow St., now the home of the Summit Hill Historical Society] and others gathered for a drink in Sweeney's Bar [corner of Ludlow & Oak Sts.] would soon find themselves entwined in a murder mystery.

Morgan Powell, Superintendent of the Lehigh Coal & Navigation Company, had a meeting scheduled with W. D. Zehner at the LC&N office located about 100 yards from the store and, together with his thirteen year old son, had stopped in Williamson's for a short visit. Although Powell was now a foreman, he had labored in the mine for several years before he was appointed inside boss at No. 2 mine and eventually appointed foreman. Talking together in Sweeney's Bar were several Irish coal miners including Thomas Fisher, Charles Mulhearn, brothers Matt and John Donohue, Robert Brislin, Phil Smith, John McHugh and Pat McKenna.

Early that evening Henry Williamson, the owner of Williamson's Store, decided to walk to his home for a short while and return to the store later. Braving the cold of the night, he left his store at 6:27 p.m. and began his short walk home. As he stepped out the door, Williamson noticed four men gathered together in the dark a few feet away from his store near Patterson's gate. [118 W. Ludlow St.] When he returned to the store at approximately 6:40 p.m., he saw only three men standing where they could look into his store and recognize anyone who was inside. He spoke to them as he passed and they answered him.

About this same time, John Cline, a master mechanic for the Lehigh Coal & Navigation Co., left Griffith Robert's Shoe Shop, just west of Williamson's store, on his way to the LC&N office [in the area of the present Spanish War Monument in the park]. As he passed Williamson's Store, Cline noticed three men standing about six or eight feet from Williamson's door between the store and the railroad and heard one man say in a loud whisper, "That's him. That's him."

At approximately 7:00 p.m., twenty minutes after Williamson returned to his store, Morgan Powell asked his son to wait at the store for his return and left the store alone, proceeding to walk east down the path along the railroad track towards Mauch Chunk [Ludlow Street]. He had walked about 20 yards when a shot pierced the night and he fell to the ground.

Samuel Allen, who lived in Summit Hill and worked in No. 8 mine, was sitting next to the door of Williamson's Store when he heard the shot and a man calling out. He immediately ran out shouting to the men in the store, *"Boys, it's Morgan Powell."* As Allen ran to the injured man lying partially on the railroad track from #1 plane and partially on the path, he called out, *"My God, Morgan, it is you."* Powell replied, *"Yes, I am shot."* Allen asked, *"Who shot you?"* Softly Powell replied, *"I don't know."* As he knelt beside Powell, Allen could hear the feet of men running away. As soon as the men in the store heard Powell had been shot, Williamson jumped over the store counter and, together with John Berian, ran out to see if they could help. Seeing the injured Powell on the railroad track, Williamson told the others to take him into the store and immediately ran a block down the footpath [Ludlow St. near Market St.] to get Dr. M. Thompson at Klotz's Hotel. George Halvey, who had been working in the LC&N office when he heard the shot, dashed out to offer assistance. Halvey, Samuel Allen and John Berian carried Powell back into Williamson's Store and propped him up on a chair. Several other men who were also nearby came running to see what had happened.

As soon as Henry Williamson returned to the store with Dr. Thompson, he quickly cleared off the counter and made a bed on it with pillows and a blanket for Powell to rest. Because Powell had become extremely pale, Dr. Thompson checked his pulse, found it very weak and intermittent, and administered a stimulant. Squire S. F. Minnick, the District Magistrate, was called and quickly arrived. During examination, Dr. Thompson noticed a wound on Powell's left side between the third and fourth ribs. By this time the store had become crowded with curious onlookers. Realizing Powell was seriously injured, the doctor asked the magistrate to clear the spectators out of the store to make the store quiet. John Berian, Robert McCready, George Halvey, Dr. Thompson, Squire Minnick and

Summit Hill
Klotz's Hotel in center
(Summit Hill Historical Society Museum)

Henry Williamson remained in the store. Morgan Price, a close friend of Powell, arrived as soon as he heard Powell had been shot.

Squire Minnick did not question Powell at first, but asked Dr. Thompson to question him. When the doctor asked Powell, *"Who shot you?"*, Powell said he believed there were three men and one man looked like Pat Gildea. When Squire Minnick asked if he knew who the other men were, Powell answered that he believed one was Blue Pat Brislin. Both Patrick Gildea and Patrick Brislin were well know to all the men. Gildea had been a corporal in the Civil War and worked as a mail agent for the Lehigh Valley Railroad in Beaver Meadow, while Brislin was a miner working in the area mines. It was known that because Brislin had been discharged from work by mine foreman Charles Powell, Morgan Powell's brother, Brislin had been searching around town for three or four days to locate Morgan Powell and ask him to intercede with his brother to get his job back.

As Squire Minnick talked with Powell, he attempted to get him to swear that Gildea and Brislin had shot him, but Powell refused to say they had been the shooters. When the Squire presented him with a Bible to swear on, Powell refused and repeatedly declined to swear that Gildea and Brislin were the men who had shot him. Powell was then asked about the third man present at the shooting and he told them a man in a long coat with a cape on it, like a soldier's overcoat, had come from behind him and shot him. The men wondered about the identity of the third man because everyone knew a man had recently quarreled with Powell at his home and either Powell or the man had drawn a knife. It was also known that as the man left Powell's house he had said, *"I will see you again."*

Surprisingly, by Sunday morning Powell's condition was slightly improved and he was not despondent, but rather hopeful. Around 4:00 p.m. the men carried Powell from the store to Morgan Price's home where he could rest more comfortably. After a short time everyone became convinced there was no hope of Powell's recovery and Dr. Leonard and Dr. DeYoung were called. As soon as they arrived Dr. Thompson noticed that Powell was suffering a great deal of pain and ordered one-quarter grain of morphine be administered to Powell. He noticed Powell's reaction time was very slow and thought Powell would pass out because the shock was becoming greater. As the doctor observed Powell's very serious condition, he knew it was necessary to obtain Powell's dying declaration. Leaning over Powell, he quietly informed him that he was in very critical condition, but did not immediately tell him he might die. Powell gave no reply to this very unsettling statement and soon the doctors left the Price home.

A few hours later District Attorney Edward F. Dimmick asked Dr. Thompson to accompany him back to the Price home to obtain from Powell an official statement as to who had shot him. Attorney Dimmick told Dr. Thompson that he, the District Attorney, would take the statement from Powell, but he wanted Dr. Thompson present to determine Powell's medical condition. Squire Minnick was also present at this time.

Upon arriving at Morgan Price's home, Dr. Thompson, District Attorney Dimmick, and Squire Minnick noticed Powell was extremely sleepy and considerably under the influence of opium. In order to arouse Powell enough for him to talk with them, Dr. Thompson found it was necessary to sprinkle cold water on his face. During the questioning Powell went to sleep two or three times and each time had to be aroused by splashing his face with water. Attorney Dimmick informed Powell he most likely would live only a few more hours and they had come to take his dying declaration. Since Powell made no reply or response to this, they were not sure if he fully comprehended his situation or what was to take place. Because of his drugged state when questioned, he answered by nod and single words, mostly "*yes*" and "*no*." After a few minutes Powell indicated he was very tired and hoped they could soon be finished. Dr. Thompson knew by this time the amount of morphine administered to

Powell that day had very likely interfered with his intellectual appreciation of his dangerous condition.

After the entire statement had been read to him, District Attorney Dimmick found Powell was unable to sign his name, but could only make an 'X' as his signature. When Powell attempted to sign, Squire Minnick held the pen and Powell touched the top of the pen. Squire Minnick commented that Powell appeared rather sleepy and under the influence of the drugs.

Between 8:00 and 9:00 a.m. on Monday December 4, 1871, Morgan Powell died. Dr. Thompson and Dr. DeYoung immediately performed a post mortem examination and extracted the ball from Powell's spinal column where it had lodged when he was shot. An inquest as to why Powell had died was held at Klotz's Hotel.

Frenzy over the murder spread rapidly throughout the community. People were determined the guilty parties should be apprehended quickly. Rewards for the capture of the murderers were quickly announced: $1,000 by the Lehigh Coal & Navigation Co., $500 by Carbon County, $200 by the Knights of Pythias of Summit Hill and $100 by the International Order of Odd Fellows. The next day the magistrate arrested Patrick Gildea and Patrick Breslin on the charge of murder.

The Grand Jury found a true bill against both Patrick Gildea and Patrick Brislin and they were indicted for murder in the first degree. [A true bill is a statement by the court that it finds evidence the accused should be prosecuted.] Although Gildea's and Brislin's counsel, Attorneys Charles Albright, Francis A. Doney and Allen Craig, appealed to the Court for the men's release on bail, Judge Dreher stated he had no authority to interfere with the action of the Grand Jury and the offense was too serious to have the men released on bail. The attorneys admitted the position of the Court was legally correct, but declared it was a harsh injustice for innocent men to be confined to jail for three months on a charge which would easily be vindicated and the men's innocence proved.

Patrick Gildea and Patrick Brislin were held in the Carbon County Jail [now the Old Jail Museum] in Mauch Chunk [Jim Thorpe] for three months and brought to trial March 1872. During their trial many witnesses told of their personal recollections and their involvement with Gildea and Brislin. The testimony of three witnesses, John Cline, Pharius Wetstone and John Churchill, proved that Gildea had been working at the time of the shooting and could not have committed the crime. Testimony of Dr. Thompson showed that Morgan Powell's final statement could not be relied upon.

John Cline: *"I am a master mechanic for the Lehigh Coal & Navigation Co. Gildea had been working at #10 slope for about three months. I had placed Pat Gildea and Pharius Wetstone in charge of the pumps which were pumping water out from #10 mine. One man was to pump by day and the other by night."*

Pharius Wetstone: *"I live in Coaldale about one-half mile from slope #10. Pat Gildea worked with me on the mine pumps keeping water out of the mine. This pump had been operating for at least three months. Normally I went to work on the night shift between 3:00 and 4:00 p.m. and worked until 4:00 or 5:00 a.m. the next morning. Gildea and me changed off every week, days and nights. I had been sick during the week and had asked Gildea to work for me during the middle of the week and Gildea did. The next day Gildea asked me if I could work for him that night and I agreed. We decided that if I worked for him that night Gildea would return the favor and work Saturday night and I did not need to come to work. From the condition of the water Saturday morning when I left the mine I felt it would have been necessary to run the pump till about 11:00 that night."*

John Churchill: *"I saw Pat (Gildea) at work in #10 on Saturday December 2. I went to work at 2:00 on Saturday. I first saw Gildea about 10 minutes after 2:00 o'clock. Don't remember seeing him again till he came out from work. I was driving a gangway at Bull Run. Me and my two laborers (Andrew Conly and Peter Sheridan) came out last. When we came to where Pat was working I said, 'Pat, you coming out'? Pat could leave early if conditions at the pump were OK. He said, 'John, if you wait a minute or two I will be with you.' As near as I can tell it was about 6:30 when we got out of the tunnel. It was 20 minutes past 7:00 when Gildea left me at my house that night. Pat then headed to Summit Hill about one mile away. He lived near St. Joseph Church."*

Dr. Thompson's testimony indicated Morgan Powell's dying statement was not reliable. *"Powell did not make a voluntary statement. If Powell been left that night to make out his own statement unassisted by our leading questions he would have been unable to make the statement. I could hardly trust the statement after the amount of morphine taken by Powell that day and would hardly consider the statement made then was valid."*

After the witnesses had completed their testimony, the Commonwealth's prosecuting attorneys retired for consultation. Upon return Attorney Dimmick announced the Commonwealth was abandoning its case against Patrick Gildea. The Court then directed the jury to acquit Gildea because the testimony of the prosecution's own witnesses had proved Gildea could not have shot Powell and, therefore, the Commonwealth had no case against him. Patrick Gildea was immediately released.

Patrick Brislin was next brought into the courtroom. After discussion the Court decided that because this was the second term of court since the arrest of Brislin and the Commonwealth was not prepared to proceed, the court would declare the defendant be discharged. Patrick Brislin was immediately released. [The law at that time demanded a defendant must be brought to trial within two terms of the court.]

After the release of Gildea and Brislin, rumors that Powell had been shot for an entirely different reason ran rampant throughout Summit Hill. It was widely known in town that Powell had been keeping company with the wife of a soldier and that the soldier was extremely angry about the situation. Many believed the man who had argued with Powell and had left Powell's home with a knife saying, *"I'll see you again,"* was this distraught husband and may have been the man who shot Powell. This rumor is described by Mark Majors in his book *Guide to the Molly Maguires*: "Morgan Powell, Superintendent of the Lehigh Coal & Navigation Co., Summit Hill, was gunned down in front of Williamson's store. . .some . . . thought a Welshman by the name of Mellin was responsible due to Powell taking up with Mellin's wife. Other sources give the man's name as Samuel Llewellyn."

Five Years Later - 1876

The search for Morgan Powell's murderer went dormant from 1871 until 1876 when Thomas P. Fisher, Alexander Campbell, John Donohue, and James McDonnell, all suspected of being members of a group of miners called Molly Maguires, were arrested and accused of the murder of Morgan Powell.

~ *Chapter II* ~

Molly Maguires

The 1800s were difficult times for Irish families. They emigrated from Ireland to escape the horrors of evictions, potato crop failure, and starvation, but found different problems in their new homeland. Widespread discrimination against the Irish was evidenced by "Help Wanted—No Irish Need Apply" signs in windows of businesses and signs saying "No Dogs—No Irish" in restaurants.

Struggling to support their families, the men found work in the coal mines, including mines in Summit Hill. Because the miners often did not live near the mine, they had to walk several miles to work and home again every day. It didn't take long for the men to realize mining was very dangerous with numerous cave-ins, fires, explosions, and accidents, all resulting in tragedy and death. The miners soon found that many weeks they were not paid a decent wage for their long hours in the dark, wet mines and, therefore, their meager pay did not cover their family's needs. Since the miners' homes were owned by the coal company, they paid the coal company rent for their homes. The men also had to buy all their food, clothing and work supplies, including picks, axes, dynamite and lumber, at inflated prices at the company-owned store. To their dismay the miners were often paid with company scrip usable only at the company store. Many weeks the miners found that after their rent and expenses were deducted from their pay they actually owed the coal company money. Once a miner was in debt to the coal company it was almost impossible for him to earn enough to pay this debt.

A miner's life was controlled by the operators of the mines who determined how much time a man would work, how much he would be paid, and how much he would be charged for his food and housing. To combat the abuses being heaped upon the miners, the Workers Benevolent Association was formed and made some advances in securing better working conditions and higher pay. The coal companies objected strenuously to these advances and soon all improvements were abruptly halted.

Outrage soon erupted across the coal region. The coal companies blamed all troubles and violence on a group of Irish miners they called the Molly Maguires. Franklin B. Gowen, President of the Philadelphia & Reading Railroad, believed that if the name Molly Maguires was mentioned in the newspapers often enough people would soon believe this organization really existed and that these men were the cause of all the problems.

Early in 1873 Franklin Gowen hired James McParlan, a detective with the Pinkerton Detective Agency, to infiltrate the so-called Molly Maguires in Carbon and Schuylkill Counties of Pennsylvania under the name of James McKenna. McParlan worked in the mines for two and one half years and reported to Gowen the activities of the suspected Mollies. The struggle for equality and the persecution of the miners continued for several years resulting in the arrest and hanging of many men as Molly Maguires.

~ Chapter III ~

Thomas P. Fisher

Born in County Donegal, Ireland, in 1837, Thomas P. Fisher came to America at the age of 12. By the time he was 22, Fisher was an outspoken opponent of the Civil War and the resulting draft.

Every citizen in the country was concerned about the possibility of war between the North and the South. Believing the war would be a short conflict, in August 1862 President Lincoln issued a call for 300,000 volunteers to serve nine months. These volunteers soon discovered their enlistment would not end in nine months, but had been extended to three years.

The new draft laws were considered unjust not only in Pennsylvania, but all across the North. Charges of class discrimination were leveled against the draft laws because it was entirely legal for a drafted man with sufficient funds to pay $300 to the government and buy a substitute or an exemption. Since $300 was the equivalent of one year's wages for most miners, they were unable to buy a substitute and had to go to war. Men reluctant to fight in the war were often forced into the ranks of the army at the point of a bayonet. This caused the war to be known as a rich man's war and a poor man's fight. The Irish immigrants also feared that the slaves made free by the war would come North and take jobs which the men desperately needed. Concern about the draft and the war invaded every aspect of life. Because the draft was resisted by numerous men, discussions and arguments were commonplace, often turning violent and erupting into fights.

In November 1862 while living in Audenried, PA, Thomas Fisher and Michael Campbell were involved in an altercation in that town's Williams Hotel, regarding the Civil War draft. A large group of men had gathered to discuss the war news and eventually the heated discussion about the draft resulted in a brawl. Both Fisher and Campbell, known to be active draft resisters, were arrested and charged with aggravated assault and battery. Each man was fined $10 and sentenced to serve fifteen months in Eastern State Penitentiary in Philadelphia. Upon appeal to the Pennsylvania Supreme Court, this decision was reversed and both Fisher and Campbell were discharged.

A few years later Fisher married and settled in Summit Hill where he worked in the mines until he lost his job during the strike in 1872. He then became the operator of the Rising Sun Hotel located on Iron St. [W. Ludlow St.] which became a popular gathering place for men who had emigrated from Ireland. Here they were able to talk with others who understood the difficulties they had left behind in Ireland and the hardships they were now facing. Fisher became active in civic affairs in Summit Hill and also became a county delegate in the Ancient Order of Hibernians [AOH], an association of Irish men dedicated to assisting Irish immigrants.

The Lehigh Wilkes Barre Coal Company [LWBC] had leased the coal lands from the Lehigh Coal & Navigation Co. [LC&N] and was operating mines on those lands. In 1874 the miners went on strike after their pay was cut by 10%. As the strike wore on, John Leisenring, Superintendent of the LC&N, realized Fisher was respected by the miners and had influence with them. He asked Fisher if he would help solve the difficulties and end the strike by meeting with Charles Parrish, the President of the LWBC, to discuss the situation and, hopefully, end the strike. Fisher agreed to a meeting in Mauch Chunk with Father Brahany and Fisher representing the strikers and Parrish representing the LWBC. This meeting became confrontational and strong words were shouted. At the end of the meeting a possible compromise was worked out between the miners and the coal company. The strike, now known as the Long Strike, ended in July 1875, after seven months.

On September 5, 1875, two months after the strike ended, LWBC mine superintendent John P. Jones was shot and killed in Lansford, PA. Alexander Campbell, age 38, Edward Kelly, age 16, and Michael Doyle, age 24, were arrested and charged with murder. Gen. Charles Albright, an attorney for the coal companies, served as prosecutor for the Commonwealth in the trials of all three men in the spring of 1876. In testimony during these trials Thomas Fisher's

Thomas P. Fisher
(Old Jail Museum Archives)

name was mentioned. When Fisher heard this he became worried his heated meeting with Charles Parrish, President of the LWBC, would somehow implicate him in the shooting of the LWBC mine superintendent, so he wrote a letter to John Leisenring explaining his concerns. Leisenring immediately delivered the letter to Albright who already knew Fisher was a defender of the striking miners and that he had been an outspoken resister of the Civil War draft.

Miner Charles Mulhearn had been involved in the violence around the mines on numerous occasions. In 1876 he was arrested in Schuylkill County and placed in the Pottsville Prison charged with conspiracy to kill brothers William and Jesse Major. Mulhearn was found guilty of conspiracy to kill the brothers, but his sentencing was postponed and he remained in the Pottsville Prison. During his trial Mulhearn's involvement in other crimes came to light and he admitted his participation in Morgan Powell's murder five years earlier. He stated in his testimony that Fisher, along with John Donohue, Patrick McKenna, and Alexander Campbell, had been involved in shooting Powell.

On September 23, 1876, a hearing on a Writ of Habeas Corpus was held before the Court of Common Pleas of Schuylkill County regarding Thomas Fisher's involvement in the murder of Morgan Powell. [A writ of habeas corpus is a hearing to determine if there is sufficient evidence to bring the accused to trial.] Even though Powell had been shot five years previously, Mulhearn was able to recall many exact details of his activities on that day. He stated that when he came home from work about 2:00 p.m. John and Matt Donohue were at his home in Newkirk, about one mile from Tamaqua. John Donohue had asked him to accompany them to Dr. Donahoe's office in Summit Hill to get medicine for his step-daughter, *"because the road was lonesome and he would be late coming back."* After Mrs. Mulhearn served them supper, the three men, John and Matt Donohue and Mulhearn, set out for Tamaqua stopping at Maley's Bar in Tamaqua for a *"couple of drinks"* and to meet Cornelius (C.T.)

McHugh, who was to lead them to Summit Hill. While they were at Maley's Bar, McHugh *"took us up to the bar and treated."* The men then continued to walk toward Summit Hill stopping again at Bridget & Barney Matthews Tavern. *"McHugh told us to go in there and have a drink."* After leaving Matthews tavern they continued walking, finally arriving at Sweeney's Bar in Summit Hill, which was very crowded with about 20 people gathered there.

Mulhearn continued his testimony: *"We went in (Sweeney's) and (John) Donohue treated. A man by the name of Frank Schwartz came in. He took us over to the bar and treated us. I think when he was done treating. . . Fisher and Pat McKenna came in. Fisher treated and we had another drink. I took a glass of porter, I think, and we had a few drinks."* Mulhearn clearly described how Pat McKenna, Phil Smith, C.T. McHugh and some other man were quarreling and fighting and, because of this disturbance, Sweeney had told them all to leave.

Although Mulhearn recalled with clarity the visits to the many bars and taverns, he could not remember whether he, the Donohue brothers, McKenna, and Fisher had walked east or west as they left Sweeney's Bar to go to the doctor's office. He stated that when they arrived at Dr. Donahoe's office the doctor was not there, so John Donohue did not get the medicine for his daughter. Mulhearn continued to describe in detail how the five men left Dr. Donahoe's office and proceeded towards Williamson's Store. He remembered that as they walked, Pat McKenna pulled a bottle out of his pocket and they had another drink. Mulhearn stated the five of them were standing near Williamson's Store when Morgan Powell was shot.

At the conclusion of the habeas corpus hearing the Commonwealth determined it had sufficient evidence against Thomas Fisher and Patrick McKenna to charge them with murder. Based mainly on the allegations of convicted murderer Charles Mulhearn, Thomas Fisher was arrested on October 19, 1876, as a participant in the 1871 murder of Morgan Powell. Capt. Robert Linden of the Coal & Iron Police, a private police force of the coal companies, sent Capt.Williams from Pottsville (Schuylkill County) to Summit Hill (Carbon County), to detain Fisher for a murder which had occurred in Carbon County. Fisher was taken back to Pottsville by the Coal & Iron Police where he was identified by Mulhearn. Fisher was then taken to the Carbon County Jail in Mauch Chunk to await his trial.

December 6, 1876

The trial of Thomas P. Fisher began with nineteen of the thirty-one prospective jurors discharged or removed. Of the twelve remaining jurors, all admitted they had read or heard about the Powell murder and about the defendants, but stated they had not formed an opinion as to Fisher's guilt or innocence. When the jury was selected, two seated jurors reported they had difficulty in understanding the English language and one juror admitted to having a hearing problem.

After raising money from his friends and relatives to pay for attorneys, Fisher secured Attorneys Edward T. Fox, John W. Ryon, and John D. Bertolette as his defense attorneys. Attorney Edward Fox had been a trial attorney for several years. Attorney John Ryon of Pottsville had been a former district attorney in Tioga County. Attorney John D. Bertolette, a Colonel in the Civil War, had passed the bar in 1867 after studying with his uncle, Gen. Charles Albright, and had been a partner in Albright's law firm for a short while.

When Thomas Fisher's attorneys realized it would be impossible for a man accused of both committing a crime and of being a Molly Maguire to obtain a fair and equitable trial in Carbon County, a change of venue was requested to move the trial to another county. Judge John P. Lavelle's book, *Hard Coal Docket,* describes the attorneys' petition for this change of venue for Fisher.

"The petition alleged

that such 'undue excitement' existed in the county against the defendants
   they could not get a fair trial;

that the jail was surrounded by armed guards to protect them from an
   'excited populace';

that because of certain inflammatory articles appearing in the newspapers of Carbon County, there was so great a prejudice against
   them as to render it impossible to get a fair trial;

that the Lehigh and Wilkes Barre Coal and Iron Company, the Philadelphia and Reading Railroad Company and others had formed a
   conspiracy to secure convictions and were expending large sums
   of money to secure their conviction;

that the private counsel retained to assist the district attorney were employed by these companies and these lawyers had employed
   special police who were 'working up' the prosecution against them;

that these lawyers had secured free trips on the railroads for witnesses
   who would testify against them;

that these companies had large and extensive operations in the county, a
   large number of the Carbon County work force is directly or indirectly dependent on these companies, and a number of the jurors
   on the panel worked for these companies; and

that the totality of these circumstances would prevent them from getting a
   fair trial."

The prosecution denied all the defendants' allegations as false and unfounded. Judge Samuel Dreher denied the request for a change of venue and the trials remained in Carbon County Court, even though the ruling completely ignored the law and the evidence.

The Commonwealth's prosecution team consisted of District Attorney Edward R. Siewers, Gen. Charles Albright, Attorney Allen Craig, and Attorney Frank H. Hughes, all prominent and experienced attorneys. Edward R. Siewers, Carbon County's District Attorney, was relatively inexperienced before the Molly trials began since he had been admitted to the bar only two years previously. As the county's District Attorney, Siewers should have been the chief counsel on this trial, but he allowed the attorneys for the coal companies and railroads to conduct the trials. Gen. Charles Albright, a close friend of Asa Packer and the chief counsel for the Lehigh & Wilkes

Barre Coal Company, became the trial's chief prosecutor. The LWBC paid Albright's salary as the trial's prosecutor. Albright was very prominent in Carbon County since he was the county's highest ranking soldier of the Civil War, having been appointed a Brevet General. He had also served in the House of Representatives for one term. Attorney Allen Craig was Asa Packer's personal attorney and chief counsel for Packer's company, the Lehigh Valley Railroad. Attorney Frank H. Hughes, was chief counsel for the Reading Railroad and had been sent by the railroad's owner, Franklin B. Gowen, to be his personal representative on this prosecution team. Hughes had an extensive legal and political background having served as Attorney General for the Commonwealth of Pennsylvania, as District Attorney for Schuylkill County for twelve years, and as a member of the United States Congress.

During the late 1800s jury members were selected from lists supplied by two jury commissioners. In those days the commissioners asked their friends, relatives and well known political people in the county to supply them with names of "sober, intelligent and judicious" men thought to make good jurors. From these lists the commissioners picked the annual pool of 600 jurors whose names were written on small papers and put in a barrel-shaped container called a jury wheel. The names of prospective jurors were then drawn from this "wheel" and given to the sheriff for each trial. Names placed into the jury pool were provided to the newspapers before the jury was selected so that everyone would know who was a possible juror.

In *Hard Coal Docket*, Judge John P. Lavelle provides details of the jury selection for the 1876 trials, including trials of the Molly Maguires, noting that only two Irishmen were selected by the jury commissioners for this jury pool. By limiting the number of Irishmen in the 600 man jury pool to two, the odds against selecting an Irish juror for a panel were overwhelming. It was not surprising that of the 211 jurors selected from the jury wheel for the panels of Fisher and other accused Molly Maguires, there was only one Irishman. Of the 72 jurors who were eventually seated for these trials, there was no Irishman among them.

Charles Mulhearn

Charles Mulhearn had been convicted of conspiracy of murder of William and Jesse Major and incarcerated in the Pottsville Prison in Schuylkill County when the prosecution requested he testify in Fisher's trial. Coal & Iron Police Capt. Linden personally transported Mulhearn from the Pottsville Prison to the Carbon County Jail where he was held during the trial. Mulhearn testified that Fisher, Alexander Campbell and several others had been participants in the shooting of Powell.

Mulhearn's memory of the shooting, which had taken place five years earlier, changed dramatically from the hearing for the writ of habeas corpus to the actual trial three months later. During the hearing he could not remember that C.T. McHugh had been waiting at Maley's Bar to lead the men to Summit Hill, but at the trial he was able to recall this. In the trial Mulhern stated that no one had talked to him and the other men gathered outside Williamson's Store even though Henry Williamson, the owner of the store, had testified he greeted the men standing there and they had replied to him. When asked during the trial which direction the men had walked after they left the doctor's office, he could not recall if they walked east or west. He also could not remember whether he had left Williamson's Store walking on a road or if he had walked on a railroad track. When asked about running to Lansford after the shooting, he could not recall if he had run "up" or "down" the inclined plane, even though Lansford was located down the mountain from Summit Hill. [The railroad track for the loaded coal cars came up the mountain from Lansford by way of the No. 1 plane. A stationary steam engine located at the top of the plane pulled the loaded coal car up the track where it was transferred to one of eight siding tracks to await the arrival of additional loaded cars. After all the loaded cars arrived, they were hooked together and sent on the down track of the Switchback Railroad where it crossed over the path [Ludlow Street] adjacent to Williamson's Store travelling to the Lehigh River at Mauch Chunk.]

The prosecution questioned Mulhearn about what he had testified during the habeas corpus hearing, but Mulhearn could not remember what he had said during that hearing three months before.

Q. Did you say at the time of the habeas corpus that you were there two hours?
A: *I don't know whether I did or not.*

Q: What time was it when Powell was shot?
A: *I don't know what time it was.*

Q: Was it true if you said so at the habeas corpus?
A: *I don't know whether I said it and I don't know what time he was shot.*

Q: If you did say so at the time of the habeas corpus, was it true or not?
A: *I don't know.*

Q: If in the hearing of the habeas corpus you said it was between 9 and 10 o'clock was that the truth?
A: *Well I don't know if I said it; it must be a mistake if I said it for I know I don't intend to tell no lies.*

James Sweeney

Many of the prosecution's questions to various witnesses pertained to the amount of time Sweeney was away from his bar and not in the company of Thomas Fisher because they needed to prove that Fisher was gone from Williamson's store the amount of time needed for him to shoot Powell and return to the store. It had been calculated by the prosecution that it would have taken a minimum of seventeen minutes for Fisher to leave Sweeney's Bar, run to Patterson's gate and meet Mulhearn, go to Williamson's store, look in the store's window and identify Powell, return to Patterson's gate and tell Mulhearn that Powell was inside the store, wait for Powell to leave, join in the shooting of Powell, run down the railroad track to No. 1 plane, return back to Sweeney's by way of White Street, [a total distance of almost 600 yards], sit and talk with Sweeney in the bar for 10 minutes and then be in the bar when Crampsey came in to tell them Powell had been shot.

In his testimony James Sweeney, the owner of Sweeney's Bar and President of Miners Savings Bank in Summit Hill, stated he remembered that Saturday night five years previously and recalled his bar had been very crowded with the usual patrons, plus several strangers. He remembered one of these unknown men had asked about the location of Dr. Donahoe's office.

Sweeney testified that he personally witnessed Fisher being in the bar and that he himself had been in the bar all evening, except for three short periods of time. He recalled that the first time he left the bar was to take drinks up to two men, Spencer and Rickert, who were in rooms on the second floor. When he came downstairs from serving the drinks, Charles McHugh, Phil Smith and one of the unknown men were fighting and he had told them to leave the bar. Sweeney said the second time he left the bar was about ten minutes later when John O'Neil, a boarder at his hotel, was found to be very intoxicated and he helped some other men take O'Neil upstairs to his room. While Sweeney was at the top of the stairs, Spencer and Rickert asked for another set of drinks. Sweeney remembered that when he came down he talked with Fisher about his boarder. Sweeney stated the third time he left the bar was when he delivered the second set of drinks to Spencer and Rickert. He testified it probably took him *"not more than a couple of minutes"* each time to go upstairs by way of the outside staircase. Sweeney also testified that while he was talking to Fisher, a young man named Crampsey came into the bar and told them Morgan Powell had been shot.

Sweeney's Bar, and bank *(corner Ludlow &
Oak Sts.)* in 1910. Today site of bank.
(Summit Hill Historical Society Museum)

The prosecution then asked Sweeney if Fisher had been in the bar at the time Powell was shot and Sweeney testified: "*After I brought down the drinks . . . I saw Fisher there and commenced talking to him about this boarder . . . I remember talking about this boarder that was unruly in liquor. Then young Gillespie came in and was sitting on the bench facing me. At this time Crampsey came in and said that Powell was shot. Fisher was talking to me at the time. . . I could not remember . . . it might be 10 or 15 minutes. . .*" The prosecution continued their attempt to show that Sweeney was out of the bar for a longer period of time than he had first stated.

Michael Crampsey

Michael Crampsey testified he had been standing outside Sweeney's Bar when he heard the shot, ran down to Williamson's Store and was inside the store when the Squire cleared everyone out. When Crampsey was asked if Fisher was at Sweeney's Bar, he said. *"No"*. When he was asked who else was at the bar that night he replied, *"I don't remember anyone who was there."*

Henry Williamson

Henry Williamson, owner of Williamson's Store, was repeatedly questioned about the men he saw the night of the shooting. He stated that when he left his store about 6:27 p.m. he *"saw four men standing near Patterson's gate. I said 'good evening', and they answered me."* He noted that when he returned to the store about 10 minutes later there were no men standing by the gate, but he saw three men standing opposite his store window where they could see inside. He said he did not know if the men he saw when he left the store were the same men he saw when he returned.

After acknowledging he had known Fisher for about 33 years and McKenna for over 15 years, Williamson was asked several times whether he recognized either Fisher or McKenna among the men outside the store. He replied, *"No sir, I did not know them."* He repeated that he had talked with Fisher and McKenna many times over the years and knew their voices, but did not recognize any voice when the men said '*good evening.*'

Capt. Robert Linden & Plea Bargains

Defendants who turned state's evidence were hoping for mercy. They had nothing to lose and everything to gain. Several prisoners charged with murder agreed to testify against Fisher and other accused miners in exchange for having their charges dropped and being freed. There was no proof of the truthfulness of these men's statements since many of them were enticed with rewards to give testimony and did not necessarily come forth on their own accord.

Kevin Kenny in his definitive book *Making Sense of the Molly Maguires* writes about the testimony of convicted prisoners who turned state's evidence and about Capt. Linden's testimony: *"It is*

Railroad St. *(Ludlow St.)* 1890
Williamson's Store is left of the trolley car.
Presently home of the Summit Hill Historical Society.
(Summit Hill Historical Society Museum)

---

impossible to know how truthful these informers were. . . would scarcely have hesitated to bend their evidence in the direction the Pinkertons required, in return for immunity from prosecution."

Capt. Robert Linden, an officer in the Coal and Iron Police and an employee of the Pinkerton Detective Agency, testified that he, Linden, had been the contact between the Pinkerton Detective Agency and the Coal & Iron Police working to incriminate the miners for trade union organizational activities, and also as Molly Maguires. When asked on whose behalf he was acting when he arrested Fisher, Capt. Linden stated it was for the National Detective Agency [Pinkerton Detective Agency].

Linden also admitted it was not unusual for him to go into a prison and propose terms to a prisoner in exchange for obtaining a confession. He acknowledged that while Mulhearn was in prison he had had at least 12 interviews with him. Linden also admitted he

Railroad St. *(Ludlow St.)* Summit Hill 1890s
Large building is the Eagles Hotel. Klotz's Hotel is in the center.
Armory is on the left. LC&N office was located directly across from the Eagles
Hotel in today's Ludlow Park. *(Summit Hill Historical Society Museum)*

had furnished Mulhearn with tobacco and had given Mrs. Mulhearn flour and other groceries. In his testimony he also stated that in the presence of Mulhearn he had ordered a doctor to visit Mrs. Mulhearn who was ill at her home. When Linden was asked who had paid for these items, he stated the National Detective Agency [Pinkertons] had supplied the money.

Under cross examination by the defense, Capt. Linden admitted that prisoners Charles Mulhearn and Cornelius T. McHugh were promised their freedom in return for cooperating. He further admitted the choice he had offered them was rather stark—either testify for the prosecution or face trial and possible execution themselves.

In addition to Charles Mulhearn, James Kerrigan, John Slattery and Cornelius McHugh all agreed to a plea bargain in order to reduce their time in prison. James (Powder Keg) Kerrigan was in prison for 19 months awaiting trial for the murder of mine superintendent John P. Jones when he was encouraged by the prosecution to testify against Fisher. Kerrigan had previously testified for the prosecution in the trials of Alexander Campbell, Michael Doyle, Edward Kelly and John Donohue who had all been found guilty and were sentenced to be hanged.

Kerrigan's written statement presented to the prosecution stated John Donohue had told him that Thomas Fisher, John Donohue and others had killed Morgan Powell. Kerrigan testified that while he was a prisoner in the Carbon County Jail [presently the Old Jail Museum] he had overheard private conversations of prisoners talking to each other through the heating system in the jail, including a conversation between Fisher and a prisoner on the second floor of the cell block. This heating system was a ducted system similar to modern air conditioning with pipes from each of the 27 cells connected to a main duct in the basement. In order to be heard, a voice would have had to travel from the heating register in a first floor cell, through the pipe down to the main pipe in the basement, across to the opposite side of the basement, and then up past the first floor to a cell on the second floor. Kerrigan offered no evidence regarding Fisher's guilt other than overheard conversations.

John J. Slattery had been charged and found guilty of conspiracy to kill the Major brothers in Schuylkill County. He turned state's evidence and agreed to testify against Fisher regarding discussions and meetings they had attended. So that he could be a prosecution witness and testify against Fisher, Slattery's sentence was delayed and he was transferred to Carbon County where he admitted that he and Mulhearn had talked together many times and that Mulhearn had told him what he was to say when he testified. Slattery also stated on the stand that he had lied in other Molly trials. He provided no definitive evidence as to Fisher's guilt.

Cornelius (C. T.) McHugh, a resident of Summit Hill, and an employee the Lehigh Coal & Navigation Company, was arrested and placed in the Carbon County Jail accused of being an accessory in the shooting of Morgan Powell. He agreed to turn state's evidence and was taken to court to testify against Fisher. In his testimony he stated that on the night of the shooting, when he had escorted the Donohues and Mulhearn from Tamaqua to Summit Hill, he had been "under the influence" before they left Tamaqua. He said that he and the others had stopped for drinks at Maley's Bar and Barney Mathews Tavern in Tamaqua and may have stopped at another bar for a drink or two before arriving at Sweeney's Bar in Summit Hill. His testimony told in detail how the men, after finally arriving at Sweeney's Bar, had several more drinks. McHugh stated he was intoxicated and had to be taken home before Powell was shot. Most of the questions asked of McHugh pertained to conversations he had had at AOH meetings during the previous months. He offered no evidence incriminating Fisher.

James McParlan

Pinkerton detective, James McParlan, had been hired by Franklin Gowen of the Philadelphia and Reading Railroad Company to act as an undercover agent in the coal regions. McParlan worked as a miner and eagerly joined the Ancient Order of Hibernians to spy on their activities. Prosecutor Charles Albright called McParlan to testify against Thomas Fisher regarding a conversation McParlan had had with Fisher in 1867. Fisher's attorneys objected to the admission of information contained in a conversation that had taken place four years before Powell had been killed, but the judge overruled the objections and permitted him to testify.

McParlan described the origin of the Ancient Order of Hibernians, its national charter, its state and local chapters and the classification of the officers. When the prosecution asked McParlan if the AOH was the same as the Molly Maguires, he replied, *"Yes,"* even though the two groups were in no way connected.

Additional Witnesses

Rev. Morton, John Bertesh and Lewis Richards testified that

at the time Powell was shot they were only a short distance from the shooting, since they were on the railroad track path which led away from the inclined plane to the area near Williamson's Store. All three men stated that after they heard the shot, they saw only three men running in their direction, not five men as Mulhearn had stated.

Many witnesses called by both the prosecution and the defense had no direct knowledge of the crime itself, but were simply residents of Summit Hill who knew or worked with Thomas Fisher.

Witnesses called for the prosecution:

C. A. Williams	Thomas McCready	John J. Slattery
Patrick Gildea	Thomas Lewis	C. Boyer
Patrick Brislin	James Edgar	Samuel Perry
John D. Churchill	George Evans	J. F. Brink
George Molvey	Thomas Arner	John Watkins
Charles Grimm	J. K. McCollum	James McParlan
C. Boyer		

Witnesses called for the defense:

Bridget Boyle	George Kent	Dr. Thomas M. Davis
Robert Klotz	John H. Harris	Frank Bynan
Abraham Tobias	John L. Friedman	John McCreay
Candy Gildea	Robert Crawford	
Edward Twining	Michael Crampsey	

Carbon County Courthouse
Mauch Chunk, PA. - 1876
(Dimmick Memorial Library)

The majority of witnesses, directly or indirectly, had earned their living from the Lehigh and Wilkes Barre Coal Company. Gen. Albright, as chief prosecutor, asked the same questions of both witnesses for the prosecution and the defense.

Q: Do you know Thomas Fisher?
A. All answered *"I know Fisher."*

Q: Do you know that Fisher was arrested for almost beating a man in Audenried?
A: *Many witnesses admitted they knew of the 1862 fight in Audenried.*

Q: Was he a member of the Molly Maguires?
A: Most replied *"Yes"*.

Q: Was he a county delegate?
A: Many answered *"Yes"*.

Gen. Albright never asked the witnesses if they knew the charges against Fisher regarding the fight in Audenried had been discharged. When asked if they knew Fisher was a county delegate, the witnesses answered *'yes'* because they knew he had been a delegate in the Ancient Order of Hibernians.

In both the hearing and the trial, the prosecution often intermixed the terms Ancient Order of Hibernians [AOH] and Molly Maguires. The Ancient Order of Hibernians was a social and civic organization of Irish men which had county delegates. The Molly Maguires was not an official organization but a name given to rebelling Irish coal miners who were alleged to be terrorists and thugs. The Molly Maguires did not have county delegates. This intermixing of the two organizations gave the impression that these two organizations were one and the same, leading a witness to believe if a man was a member of one organization, he was automatically a member of the other. While it was true that many men accused of

Hanging of Thomas P. Fisher
Main cell block of the Carbon County Jail in Mauch Chunk
March 28, 1878

(Old Jail Museum Archives)

being Molly Maguires were also members of the AOH, every member of the AOH was not a Molly Maguire. By intermixing these two terms, the prosecution was effectively implying that Fisher, as a member of the AOH, was automatically a Molly Maguire and, therefore, was a dangerous and disreputable person capable of murder.

Thomas Fisher was not permitted to testify in his own defense.

December 16, 1876
After discussing the case for only four hours the jury found Thomas P. Fisher guilty of murder in the first degree of Morgan Powell in 1871. James McKenna was found guilty of murder in the second degree in the death of Morgan Powell and sentenced to be imprisoned in Eastern State Penitentiary for nine years.

Two days later
Attorneys for Thomas Fisher immediately began the process of saving his life by filing a motion for a new trial.

January 1877
Motion for new trial withdrawn.

June 14, 1877
Death warrant issued fixing August 8, 1877, as the date of execution.

June 28, 1877
Writ of Error **[A writ of error is used to review the judgment of a lower court or to correct an error of fact]** was taken out removing the case to the Supreme Court. This required the death warrant to be withdrawn. Fisher's attorneys now had until October 1 when the Supreme Court was to meet to save him.

October 1, 1877
Supreme Court met and issued a new death warrant fixing February 26, 1878, as the date of Fisher's execution.

February 1, 1878

Affidavit of James Sweeney presented to Governor Hartranft appealing for clemency for Fisher. After due consideration of Sweeney's affidavit, the Governor granted a 30 day reprieve for Fisher and also granted him another hearing before the Board of Pardons.

The contents of Sweeney's secret affidavit had become known to the prosecution. An informer, possibly either Charles Mulhearn or James Kerrigan who had both testified for the prosecution, met with a reporter for the *Carbon Democrat* and discussed Sweeney's affidavit. This conversation, published in the newspaper, indicated that the informer had stated James Sweeney was a member of the Molly Maguires and he should be concerned because he could possibly be now considered an accessory to Morgan Powell's murder.

After these affidavits appeared in the newspaper Sweeney immediately appeared before the magistrate and "corrected" some of the contents of his original affidavit indicating he might be in error in judging the amount of time he had been gone from his bar.

Fisher had been in prison for eighteen months and watched and prayed for eight months as his attorneys filed numerous appeals to save him from execution. During the last few weeks, hope gradually but surely slipped from his grasp. The date of his execution was set for March 28, 1878.

February 15, 1878

One month before Fisher was to be hanged the following notice appeared in the newspaper, but was never presented to the court:

Valley Gazette
Charles McShea, a prisoner in the Carbon County Jail at the time of these trials stated John (Yellow Jack) Donahue told him Thomas Fisher was innocent of the Morgan Powell crime. McShea said he will make an affidavit before the magistrate to this fact.

~ *Chapter IV* ~

Execution Day

March 28, 1878

Well before 9:00 a.m. people began to gather at the Carbon County Jail on West Broadway in Mauch Chunk in anticipation of the hanging of Thomas P. Fisher. The number of people outside the prison was so great that many of them had little hope of getting inside to attend the hanging. Pushing and shoving, the crowd moved against the iron railing on the prison's front steps bending it in such a way that it was in danger of breaking and allowing people to fall into the street below.

Reporters from both local and city newspapers around the country had come to cover this gruesome story. Huddling together in the rain, the reporters applauded when the sheriff began to call the jurors to enter because they knew they would soon get into the prison. As soon as all deputies, jurors and reporters had entered the giant wooden doors, an announcement was made for those 300 people to whom tickets had been issued to enter the building. One reporter from the *Mauch Chunk Democrat* squeezed through the dense crowd inside only to find there was no way to get close to the gallows. When he tried to go up the stairs to the second level of the cell block, he found his way blocked by the Coal & Iron Police. Using his press credentials as a pass, he finally got to the upper extreme rear of the jail where he could look down on the instrument of death.

Reproduction Gallows in the Old Jail Museum
Jim Thorpe, PA.
In exact location of original gallows

(Old Jail Museum Archives)

In the solitude of his cell, Father Bunce of Mauch Chunk and Father Wynne of Summit Hill prayed with Fisher. They knelt alongside the solemn prisoner with Sheriff Raudenbush and two officers kneeling and holding candles. Pale and emaciated, Fisher followed the prayers silently. Soon the prearranged signal was given to begin the execution. Tightly grasping an ebony and gold crucifix in both hands, Fisher walked forward with a firm, unshaken step and placed himself beside the sheriff. Holding candles and prayer books in their hands, the two priests walked behind Fisher as the solemn procession moved towards the gallows. All the time the sheriff and his assistants were shackling Fisher's ankles and handcuffing his hands, he never ceased praying.

Fisher slowly mounted the scaffold in silence and prayer, accompanied by the priests whispering words of consolation. When all reached the top platform, the sheriff asked Fisher if he had anything to say. Fisher slowly opened a folded paper. Casting his eyes over the crowd assembled below, he read in a low, but distinct, voice so that almost every word was heard:

> **"I am innocent of the Powell murder and never conspired against him. I never offered any reward for his death. I never plotted his death. I was in Sweeney's Hotel the night of the murder. A little boy came in and told it to me. I ran out and then came in again; then Rapsher told me about the murder. This is not all I have to say but I don't want to take up your time. I die innocent of the murder and forgive everyone that has injured me and if I have injured anyone I hope they will forgive me."**

Sheriff Raudenbush, his assistants and the two priests knelt on the floor of the scaffold. Fisher, whose eyes were raised upward, prayed unceasingly as the priests read passages from their prayer books. The sheriff then prepared to do his duty. A white bag was carefully pulled down over Fisher's face and the noose placed around

his neck and tightened. Everyone left the platform a~ ~d Fish~~
left alone on the scaffold. At 10:57 a.m. the assigned ~~~~ ~~
The signal for the opening of the gallows floor was ~.
fateful drop occurred.

As Fisher died on the gallows, Dr. DeYoung and Dr. Erwin checked his pulse and heart at regular intervals. It was recorded that Fisher's last heart beat was noticed at 11:09 a.m., twelve and one-half minutes after the floor of the gallows had opened. His body was permitted to hang on the gallows for one-half hour and was then cut down by Sheriff Raudenbush. Upon examination of his body by the physicians, it was found that Fisher's neck had been broken. The Summit Hill undertaker immediately placed Fisher's lifeless body into an ice box. Manus O'Donnell, Andrew Meehan, Walt Conway, and Patrick Mulhearn, along with two other men, solemnly carried Fisher to the hearse waiting in front of the prison.

On Broadway in front of the jail, a procession was formed of the hearse containing Fisher's body, a double carriage carrying James Sweeney and several other people, a single buggy with Fisher's brother and nephew, and a wagon with six people followed by over 100 persons silently walking behind the vehicles. The procession moved solemnly and quietly up West Broadway out of Mauch Chunk toward Summit Hill, a walk of about eight miles.

Many sympathizers had remained in front of the prison during the hanging, together with many curious onlookers. After Fisher's body was removed from the prison, the large wooden doors of the prison were opened and a continuous stream of people packed themselves into the cell block to view the instrument of death upon which eight persons had died. [Five men had been hanged on this gallows in the Carbon County Jail and three men had died on it in Bloomsburg, Pa.]

It was originally intended that Fisher would be buried the following Sunday at St. Joseph Church in Summit Hill, but Father

Wynne had previously planned the traditional Forty Hours Devotion for that day so the funeral had to be changed to Saturday. At 3:00 p.m. on that gloomy day, an extremely large crowd of mourners from many parts of Carbon and Schuylkill County gathered at Fisher's home in Summit Hill in preparation for the funeral. The newspaper estimated that over 502 persons were present at the funeral service conducted by Father Wynne at St. Joseph Church. After the funeral John McHugh, William Shay, Edward Boyle and William Boyle solemnly carried the casket containing Fisher's body to his grave site in the rear of the church.

The following day, the sad details of Fisher's death were reported in the *Coal Gazette.*

Coal Gazette   **March 29, 1878**
The Execution
The body swung around and about a minute after the drop the limbs moved slightly. At six and a half minutes there was a convulsive shudder of the whole frame. At 11-1/2 minutes pulsation ceased, and one minute later the heart ceased to beat and Thomas P. Fisher was a dead man. The body was allowed to hang 32 minutes and was lowered in the coffin.

Although Thomas Fisher had not been permitted to testify at his trial, his final statement of innocence, which included Fisher's description of the events at Sweeney's Bar the night Morgan Powell was shot, was printed in the newspaper the day after his execution.

Coal Gazette   **March 29, 1878**
I came right into Sweeney's. Five Minutes had not elapsed from the time I went out until I came in. That was the only time I was outside of Sweeney's from the time I came there early in the evening until I left about nine or half after nine o'clock. When I came in I got talking to Sweeney about the fuss that occurred with McKenna and one of his boarders. We talked together some time. I went up to the bar and called

for a treat. . . Sweeney waited on us. I do not know how many there were, four or five drank. . . After the treat Sweeney and I got talking about the fuss and exchanging views on many subjects, when a small boy came in and said Powell was shot. At this time I was standing by the heater and remember well that Sweeney was there. . . Fifteen or twenty minutes afterwards Crampsie came in and said Powell was shot. Sweeney and I were standing at the heater and we did not hardly believe him.

On April 5, 1878, one week after Thomas Fisher was hanged, the *Coal Gazette* printed a statement by Manus Kull, also known as Kelly the Bum. In this statement Kull declared that Thomas P. Fisher was innocent of the Powell murder.

Coal Gazette   April 5, 1878

Had the fact of the statement been published before Fisher's death, it might have had an important bearing on his fate.

Kelly the Bum was arrested and lodged in the Schuylkill County prison on some minor charge. While there Alexander Campbell visited him and in talking over matters confidentially, Kelly asked Campbell if Tom Fisher had anything to do with the Powell murder. Campbell answered that Fisher had nothing to do with the crime at all. This answer may have been given by Campbell in an off hand way to stop Kelly's questioning and it may have been true. Alec Campbell knew all about the murder and who were engaged in it, that is certain.

Whatever may have been the facts as to Fisher's guilt or innocence, we believe that he had no idea that he would be charged with the murder of Morgan Powell when he was arrested.

~ Chapter V ~

Hand of Innocence

In the years following his execution, an intriguing legend regarding Thomas Fisher has emerged. This legend, described by several writers, states that before his hanging Fisher made a startling prediction, both parts of which have come true:

*"A century from now this Mauch Chunk Prison will
be an historic landmark. I am innocent. When the
day of my execution comes I will let the public know
that I am an innocent man."*

The first part of this prediction was fulfilled in 1974, ninety-six years after Fisher died, when the Carbon County Jail in Jim Thorpe was registered on the National Register of Historic Places, U.S. Department of Interior.

The second part of the prediction came true on the night before his hanging when Fisher placed his hand on the wall of his prison cell saying, *"My mark will stay here as long as this prison remains as a sign of my unjust execution."* Fisher's hand print on the cell wall today remains visible as proof of his innocence as he predicted.

The first record of the mysterious hand print is in a delightful 1884 oral history. Mary Siegel Tyson's book, *The Miners,* tells of

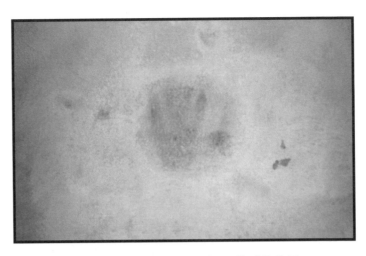

Mysterious handprint on the wall of Cell 17
in the Old Jail Museum, Jim Thorpe

(Old Jail Museum Archives)

her grandparents' lives in the coal region of northeast Pennsylvania. One interesting tale is of an outing her grandparents took to the Wahnetah Hotel and the falls of Glen Onoko along the west bank of the Lehigh River near Mauch Chunk. *"They did not stop at the dancing pavilion... but rather, they joined other curious excursionists on their way to visit the Mauch Chunk jail. There, on the wall of one of the cells, the imprint of a hand was clearly visible. . . .His name was Fisher — Thomas Fisher. His father was a Pennsylvania Dutchman and his mother was Irish."* When the young girl asked the warden why he didn't just white-wash over the mark, the warden replied, *"Since his execution we've white-washed over that wall many times, but the hand always reappears."* Quickly the girl replied, *"Let's get out of here. This place gives me the creeps."*

In an October 28, 1975, Jim Thorpe Sheriff Louis Lisella stated in the *National Enquirer, "The night before his execution a known member of the Molly Maguires told the sheriff that Fisher had had no part in the killing. The sheriff telegraphed the Governor, but the message was ignored. That was the night Tom Fisher, in deep bitterness, put his hand against the wall and left the print."* In the same article, prison Warden Richard Cochran said, *"I can't explain it. I've studied the print closely and had the guards try to wash it off the wall without success. It's been painted over a number of times— but still comes back a few days later. Nobody has been able to explain it in nearly 100 years."*

In October 1975 the *National Inquirer* commissioned a scientific investigation of this strange phenomenon. Dr. Jeffrey T. Cline, a geologist, of Wilkes College in Wilkes-Barre, PA., examined the hand print. Samples of the hand print and wall were analyzed in a gas chromatograph, a device used to determine the chemical composition of organic materials. The analysis showed no trace of grease whatsoever, only the paint on the wall showed in the test results. He stated, "If the print is not a grease mark, then there is no logical explanation for its persistence on the wall."

In recent years, two people visiting the Old Jail Museum remembered incidents from their childhood regarding the mysterious hand print on the wall. Both visitors distinctly recalled eagerly accompanying their grandfather to the Carbon County Prison after he had been asked to remove the hand print from the cell wall. These people stated they also remembered that after their grandfather removed the hand print he was called again the following day to come back to the prison because the hand print had reappeared.

The mysterious hand print on the wall of Cell 17 is today visible to all who visit the Old Jail Museum in Jim Thorpe.

~ *Chapter VI* ~

Reasonable Doubt

A fter reading more than 1,100 handwritten pages of the original trial transcripts and spending countless hours looking at microfilms of old newspapers in the Dimmick Memorial Library, a strong 'reasonable doubt' arose that Thomas P. Fisher was not guilty of the murder of Morgan Powell and may have been unjustly hanged. Here are just some of the unresolved issues which brought about the reasonable doubt.

Issue 1
No real evidence was presented and no motive revealed to prove Fisher was guilty of the murder of Morgan Powell.

Issue 2
Charles Mulhearn's statements implicating Thomas P. Fisher in the shooting of Morgan Powell were the only evidence against Fisher and are questionable for several reasons:

a) The statements were made during Mulhearn's own trial for attempted murder.

b) Mulhearn acknowledged in court that Coal & Iron Police Capt. Robert Linden had talked with him in prison at least 12 times before he testified.

c) Mulhearn's alcohol impaired condition at the time of the shooting would have made him unable to recall events with certainty, yet his statements were accepted. He freely admitted he had taken a minimum of ten alcoholic drinks in the three hour period before Powell was shot. Although no one knows Mulhearn's exact weight, we can presume he was of average size, about 5' 8" weighing about 165 lbs. According to the current Pennsylvania Liquor Control Board's Alcohol Impairment Chart, a man of this size consuming 10 drinks in three hours would result in an approximate blood alcohol level of between .16% and .19% and would have had a drastic effect on him by altering his memory, reasoning, and hearing. At that stage he would have been considered grossly impaired with his judgement and perception severely diminished. If he had weighed 180 lbs. he would have been only slightly less intoxicated.

Issue 3

Many witnesses changed their testimony from one Molly Maguire trial to the next in order to suit the goal of the prosecution—find the defendant guilty. It has been a real challenge to put into order the statements made by each witness at each trial, because the same person often gave contradictory information about an incident. Was this because of poor memory or because the prosecution had encouraged the witnesses to change their testimony?

Issue 4

Based on Gen. Charles Albright's own statement, the fact that Fisher had been a known draft resister meant Albright considered him a traitor. Having received the rank of Brevet General in the Civil War, Albright firmly believed everyone who was not in favor of the war was a traitor to his country and should be dealt with accordingly. A speech he had delivered in Mauch Chunk during the war years expressed this strong personal belief. *"My country first; my country last; and my country all the time, right or wrong! Death to traitors now and forever."*

Issue 5

Gen. Albright's numerous efforts to influence the jury, without presenting actual evidence, were exhibited in numerous ways:

a) Gen. Albright wore his Civil War uniform, including his sword, in the courtroom as he acted as prosecutor even though the Civil War had been over for 10 years.

b) Albright's intermixing of the terms Ancient Order of Hibernians (AOH) and Molly Maguires implied to the jury that all members of the AOH were also members of the notorious Molly Maguires.

c) Albright obviously intended to overwhelm the jury with numbers by calling to the stand a large number of witnesses who had no knowledge of the crime and could add nothing to the case except a personal acquaintanceship with Fisher.

d) The manner in which Albright repeatedly questioned witnesses about their knowledge of Fisher's involvement in a fight which had occurred 13 years before Powell was shot implied that Fisher was a troublemaker. *"Is it not so that Fisher almost killed a man and was sent to a state penitentiary?"* He never mentioned to the jury that this past charge against Fisher had been dismissed.

e) Albright would have had an unfair advantage over the prosecution with knowledge of testimony and details in the shooting since had been a defense attorney in the previous trials of Patrick Gildea and Patrick Brislin for the murder of Morgan Powell.

Issue 6

The prosecution did not prove that Fisher was gone from Sweeney's Bar the amount of time required for him to shoot Powell and return to the bar.

Issue 7

The Commonwealth never investigated the possibility that the men standing outside Williamson's Store were the actual murderers of Morgan Powell. Although several witnesses stated the men gathered outside the store were there from 6:27 p.m., when Williamson left to go home, until 7:05 p.m., when Powell was shot, this was not investigated.

Issue 8

The identity of the fourth man standing outside Williamson's Store, and the possibility that this man was Powell's killer, were never investigated by the Commonwealth even though Powell had said he was shot by someone wearing a soldier's overcoat and it had been rumored that Powell was involved with the wife of a soldier.

Issue 9

The possibility that only three men, not five, were involved in the shooting was never investigated. The testimony of Rev. Morton, John Bertsch and Lewis Richards that they saw only three men running past them immediately after the shooting, not five men as Mulhearn stated, indicated the two Donohues and Mulhearn may have been running from the shooting and would have eliminated Fisher and McKenna from being at the shooting.

Issue 10

Henry Williamson did not recognize Fisher as being one of the men he saw on his way home or returning to his store the night of the shooting, even though he knew Fisher for over 30 years and knew the sound of his voice.

Issue 11

Inmates in the Carbon County Jail would have been very unlikely to incriminate themselves in conversations that could have been overheard by prisoner James Kerrigan, since he was known as a turncoat who had testified at several previous trials of accused Molly Maguires who were found guilty.

Issue 12

The defense never raised the possibility that Pinkerton Detective James McParlan, who had been hired by the coal companies as their spy in the coal regions, may have passed on defense strategy to the prosecution. McParlan had been the star prosecution witness in the trials of accused Molly Maguires Michael Doyle and Edward Kelly, and therefore had knowledge of defense tactics used in other trials of men accused of being a Molly Maguire.

Issue 13

Thomas Fisher was not permitted to testify in his own defense. The only statements heard from Fisher were those he made to newspapers and printed after his death.

You have read the testimony of Thomas P. Fisher's trial and heard about the mysterious hand print on the wall of Cell 17. It's now time to come to your own conclusion.

Was Thomas P. Fisher an active participant in the shooting of Morgan Powell?

Should Thomas P. Fisher have died on the gallows?

Or,

Do you have a serious doubt as to Thomas P. Fisher's guilt in the shooting of Morgan Powell?

Participants

Gen. Charles Albright

Two months after Fisher's trial, Charles Albright served as prosecutor in the trials of Charles Sharpe and James McDonnell, the last Molly Maguire trials in which he was the prosecutor. He had been the prosecutor in eight Molly Maguire trials between January 1876 and September 1878. In seven of these cases the defendants were found guilty and sentenced to death by hanging. The eighth defendant received a sentence of four years in a state penitentiary. Charles Albright died in 1880 at the age of 50 after choking on food and entering into a coma.

Charles Mulhearn

Two weeks after Fisher was hanged, Charles Mulhearn testified against Charles Sharpe and James McDonnell, accused of the 1863 murder of George K. Smith and of being Molly Maguires. After testifying, he was granted his release from prison. Charles Sharpe and James McDonnell died on the gallows on January 14, 1879.

James Kerrigan

Two weeks after Fisher was hanged, James Kerrigan testified against Charles Sharpe and James McDonnell, accused of the murder of George K. Smith. After testifying, he was granted his release from prison. The Carbon County Commissioners gave Kerrigan a promissory note in the amount of $1,000 to be redeemed one year later. No reason was given for the presentation of the funds. James Kerrigan moved south with his wife and lived under his wife's maiden name.

Cornelius McHugh and John Slattery

After testifying against Fisher charges against Cornelius McHugh and John Slattery were dropped and they were released from prison
.

James McParlan

James McParlan, born in County Armagh, Ireland, was an employee of the Pinkerton Detective Agency. He was chosen to infiltrate the

Molly Maguires as a spy and was a main witness in the trials of men accused of being Molly Maguires. His testimony in several cases was unsubstantiated by other testimony or positive evidence, and many times his testimony only repeated the statements of others who had turned state's evidence in order to receive their freedom from prison. After the Molly trials ended, McParlan was assigned by the Pinkertons to infiltrate the gold mines in Colorado in order to bring an end to the unions. The tactics he had used in the trials of the Molly Maguires were later exposed by Attorney Charles Darrow in the 1907 murder trial of Idaho ex-governor Frank Steunenberg. Darrow's outstanding defense of the union men in that trial revealed exactly what McParlan had done in the Molly Maguire trials. James McParlan died in 1919 at 75 years of age a victim of ill health and alcoholism.

Franklin B. Gowen

Franklin B. Gowen, President of the Philadelphia and Reading Railroad and the Philadelphia and Reading Coal & Iron Company, worked closely with Asa Packer, Lehigh Valley Railroad, and Charles Parish, Lehigh & Wilkes-Barre Coal Company, to control coal production and transportation. He was instrumental in the arrests and trials of all accused Molly Maguires. In December 1889 Franklin Gowen was found dead in a Washington, D.C., hotel room from an apparent suicide.

Charles Parrish

Charles Parrish was the president of the Lehigh Wilkes-Barre Coal Company. He went bankrupt in 1878 and died one year later.

Asa Packer

Asa Packer was President of the Lehigh Valley Railroad. He died suddenly in 1879.

Allen Pinkerton

Allen Pinkerton, President of the Pinkerton Detective Agency, had a stroke after Alexander Campbell's execution in 1877. By 1880 he was becoming incoherent. Four years later he was senile and died from a massive stroke.

Ancient Order of Hibernians
Founded in 1836, the Ancient Order of Hibernians (AOH) is a fraternal organization whose members are Catholic men born in Ireland or are of Irish descent. Their motto is *"Friendship, Unity, Christian Charity"*. Formed to defend the Catholic Church and give aid and help to Irish immigrants, the members also secured food, housing and assistance for families of members killed in the mines. Today members are involved in widespread charities and missions.

Molly Maguires
Molly Maguires was a name given to Irish coal miners working diligently, and often violently, to better conditions in the mines and to protect their employment. In the 18th century, Ireland was home to the Defenders, a secret society that punished landlords who abused their Irish tenants and evicted many struggling Irish families from their homes. The name Molly Maguires is said to have originated with a woman from County Cavan, Ireland, who either led a band of Defenders or was sympathetic to their cause and hid members on the run. When the miners began to organize to improve conditions, they were called the "Sons of Molly Maguire." There is no known connection between Molly Maguire of Ireland and the miners called the sons of Molly Maguire, except for their fight for justice and equality.

St. Joseph Cemetery
Thomas P. Fisher was laid to rest in St. Joseph Catholic Church Cemetery in Summit Hill, PA., along with Alexander Campbell, Hugh McGeehan, and James Boyle, all accused Molly Maguires. There are no monuments or stones standing for any person buried in this cemetery. It has been rumored that years ago all tombstones were leveled and covered with dirt because vandals were continually defacing the tombstones of the Molly Maguires. The cemetery today is a grassy setting of peace and memory.

References

Thomas E. McBride
> Commonwealth vs. Patrick Gildea
> Commonwealth vs. Patrick Brislin
> Commonwealth vs. Thomas P. Fisher

Dimmick Memorial Library, Jim Thorpe, PA.
> Microfilm Collection of Newspapers

Hard Coal Docket
> John P. Lavelle, 1994

Making Sense of the Molly Maguires
> Kevin Kenny, Oxford University Press, 1998

Guide to the Molly Maguires, A
> H. T. Crown, Mark T. Major, 1995

Mauch Chunk Switchback, The
> Vincent Hydro, Jr.
> Canal History & Technology Press 2002

Old Jail Museum

The original Carbon County Prison at 128 West Broadway in Mauch Chunk is today known as the Old Jail Museum, Jim Thorpe, PA. It served as the Carbon County Prison from 1871 until January 1995. The name of the small town of Mauch Chunk was changed to Jim Thorpe in 1954.

Resembling a fortress standing guard over the town, the historic two story jail was constructed in 1871 with thick, massive, hand cut stone walls and a formidable tower.

Old Jail Museum
Jim Thorpe, PA.
(Old Jail Museum Archives)

The entire front portion of the building served as the warden's living quarters from 1871 until 1970, complete with a living room, dining room and kitchen on the first floor and three bedrooms and bathroom on the second floor. The prison component of the building consisted of 27 cells in the first floor main cell block, 16 eerie, solitary confinement cells in the basement dungeon, and three women's cells on the second floor.

The ornamental, cast iron railing around the front of the building is formed in the pattern of a knotted rope, so even the fence served as a symbol of confinement. This outside railing and the beautiful railing on the second floor tier of cells were both constructed at the Albright & Stroh Foundry in Mauch Chunk, which was originally owned by Gen. Charles Albright. The beautiful, ivy-covered stone wall that once encased the building was partially removed in 1970 and replaced with wire fencing.

Cell 17 contains the mysterious hand print placed on the wall by Thomas P. Fisher as proof of his innocence. Over the past 135 years the jail's many wardens have tried to eliminate the hand print by washing it, painting over it and even removing the plaster.

In January 1995 the jail was purchased from Carbon County by Thomas E. and Betty Lou McBride, residents of Jim Thorpe. After extensive washing and scrubbing, the Old Jail Museum, a non-profit enterprise, opened to visitors in May 1995.

The Old Jail Museum, an excellent example of 19th century prison architecture, is listed on the National Register of Historic Buildings. Each year the Old Jail is delighted to have visitors from all 50 states and from at least 24 foreign countries. History and mystery continue to abound in the Old Jail Museum.

See you in Jail - *the Old Jail, of course.*

❧ TOURS ❧

Memorial Day Weekend through Labor Day
Daily: 12:00 noon to last tour at 4:30 p.m.
Closed Wednesday
Weekends only September & October
Closed for the winter November through May

Old Jail Museum
128 W. Broadway
Jim Thorpe, PA 18229
570-325-5259

www.TheOldJailMuseum.com
e-mail: TheOldJailMuseum@verizon.net

~ About the Authors ~

Thomas E. McBride was born in Hazleton, PA. of Irish and Welsh heritage. Tom learned firsthand the challenges of life in the coal region. After spending many years as a Realtor in Naples, FL, Tom returned to the coal region in 1981, relocating to Jim Thorpe, PA, with his wife, Betty Lou, and their three daughters. Recognizing the beauty and vast potential of the yet-to-be-revived town of Jim Thorpe, Tom restored a decaying Victorian building in downtown Jim Thorpe and opened the Treasure Shop, a general gift and Irish import store. In 1995 Tom and Betty Lou purchased the Carbon County Prison and opened it to the public as the Old Jail Museum. Tom's first book, *Civil War Draft Resistance and the Molly Maguires*, has been well received and is noted for its historical information on the Molly Maguires.

Betty Lou Kemmerling McBride, was born in Cleveland, Ohio, and worked for many years as a legal secretary and office manager. After Betty Lou and Tom married in 1968, they resided in Naples, FL, for 13 years. When the family moved to Jim Thorpe, she joined with Tom in establishing the Treasure Shop and the Old Jail Museum. An established author, Betty Lou has written two additional books, *The Old Jail Museum and the Molly Maguires,* and the *Ghosts of the Molly Maguires?*